Solving for Success: Crafting
Wealth through Numerical Wisdom

Thomas H. Sullivan

# Introduction

Welcome to "Solving for Success: Crafting Wealth through Numerical Wisdom." To illustrate the transformative power of numerical insights, let me introduce you to Emma and Alex, two friends with different approaches to their financial lives.

Emma and Alex both started their careers at the same company, earning similar salaries. Emma was passionate about her work but found herself living paycheck to paycheck, often struggling to make ends meet. She believed that financial success was reserved for those with high incomes or extraordinary luck.

Alex, on the other hand, had a different perspective. He saw numbers not as daunting figures but as tools for crafting his financial future. From a young age, he was fascinated by how small numerical changes could lead to significant financial outcomes. He spent time learning about budgeting, saving, and investing, and approached his finances with the precision of an engineer solving a complex problem.

One day, Emma confided in Alex about her financial struggles. After giving careful attention, Alex explained his strategy.He explained how he set clear financial goals, meticulously tracked his income and expenses, and made informed investment decisions. Emma was intrigued but skeptical. How could understanding a few numbers make such a difference?

Alex offered to help Emma apply the same principles to her finances. They started with the basics: crafting a balanced budget and setting realistic savings goals. Alex showed Emma how to use compound interest to her advantage and introduced her to simple investment strategies that aligned with her risk tolerance.

As Emma began to implement these changes, she noticed a gradual but undeniable transformation. Her anxiety about money decreased, and she started to see her savings grow. Inspired by her progress, Emma continued to delve deeper into the world of financial numbers, learning how to optimize her taxes and manage debt effectively.

Fast forward a few years, and Emma's financial situation had dramatically improved. She had not only achieved financial stability but was also well on her way to building lasting wealth. The once-daunting numbers had become her allies, guiding her toward financial success.

"Solving for Success: Crafting Wealth through Numerical Wisdom" is designed to guide you on a similar journey. Through the pages of this book, you'll discover how to decode the numbers that govern your financial decisions, set clear and achievable goals, and implement strategies that will lead to lasting prosperity.

This isn't just a book about numbers; it's about transforming your relationship with money and empowering you to take control of your financial destiny. Like Emma, you'll learn to see the beauty in the numbers and unlock the secrets they hold.

So, let's embark on this journey together. Open your mind to the possibilities that numerical wisdom offers, and prepare to transform your financial future. Welcome to "Solving for Success." Your path to financial mastery begins here.

# CHAPTER 1: Understanding Financial Equations

It is crucial to understand how to use some of the standard financial formulae to assess the success of your finances, whether you are examining your personal accounts or those of a business. It should be evident to you that you are making a healthy profit on your investments and that you are not going beyond your means. However, it might be challenging to determine your true position if you are unaware of how such computations are done. Here is a useful financial formula sheet as a result.

We may assist you if you require an understanding of finance math formulae for personal or academic purposes. The most frequent formulae that you will need to comprehend are covered in the following sections, along with clear, concise explanations and examples.

### The Operating Cash Flow Formula

It's critical to comprehend your cash flow if you wish to avoid running into major issues. To ensure that you are constantly making more money than you are spending, it is desirable to have an income that is higher than your costs. You should certainly try to avoid spending more money than you make, which is indicated by a negative cash flow figure. You have extra money when there is a positive cash flow, which you may put aside or, better yet, invest to bring in more money. The operating cash flow formula, which is simple to learn and comprehend, is as follows:

The operating cash flow formula, which is simple to learn and comprehend, is as follows: Income - Expenses equals cash flow.

Therefore, your monthly cash flow is as follows: $2500 - $2250 = $250 if your costs are $2250 and your income is $2500.

To achieve a better and more accurate metric, cash flow should always be calculated over an extended period of time. This is so that you account for potential yearly costs like insurance and make allowances for any fluctuations in your income due to the seasons or other factors.

**Leverage ratio: What Is It?**

The utilization of borrowed funds, or debt, is known as leverage. Whether it's an overdraft, a car loan, or a mortgage, the majority of people and companies also have debt. What matters is that your debt should not be excessive in relation to your income.

Your leverage ratio may be calculated as follows: Leverage Ratio = Debt Payments ÷ Income

Based on your monthly income of $3000 and the $750 you pay off in debt, your leverage ratio comes out to be $750 ÷ $3000 = 0.25 or 25%.

Maintaining your leverage ratio at less than 33% of your normal revenue is often the wisest course of action. The smaller the ratio, the more protected you are against facing a financial setback like being laid off.

**Ratio of Leverage Using Equity**

You may compute your leverage in relation to your equity as well. For example, if the value of your home or place of business is $500,000 and you owe $200,000 on it as a mortgage, your equity is $300,000.

Here's the method to find your leverage ratio in relation to equity: Total debt ÷ Total equity is the leverage ratio.
Accordingly, our equity leverage ratio for the above-quoted amounts is $200,000 ÷ $300,000 = 0.67, or 67%.

The more secure you are, the lower you maintain this ratio. This is frequently used as a gauge of your existing level of risk and needs to be taken into account before making any new investments or other adjustments.
Finding the Gains or Losses in Your Market

You want the value of everything you purchase as an investment, like stocks or real estate, to improve so that you have more equity.

You may use the following calculation to see how much you have gained or even lost: (Market Price - Purchase Price) ÷ Purchase price is the percentage increase.

Given that equities were purchased for $6 and are now worth $10, your returns would be as follows: ($10 – $6) ÷ $6 = 67% gain.

The percentage loss on your investment would be represented as a negative number in this case, which is obviously something you want to avoid.

## How to Calculate Financial Success

Understanding how to enhance a company's fiscal performance begins with having a comprehensive view of its fiscal status and creating a budget. Measure cash inflow, net income, and other small company performance measures to discover openings for enhancement. Common stylish practices include reducing business expenditures and modifying payment terms to insure prompt collection of accounts delinquent. Other frequent strategies for perfecting fiscal performance include dealing firm means, raising pricing, giving markdowns to shift fat force, and consolidating debt.

## 5 fiscal Performance Measures to Cover

**1. Gross profit periphery:** Gross profit periphery is a profitability statistic that calculates the proportion of profit remaining after abating the cost of goods vended. The cost of products vended is the direct cost of the product, which excludes functional expenditures, interest, and levies. In other words, gross profit periphery is a measure of profitability for a given product or item line that doesn't include overhead costs.

Gross Profit periphery = ( profit- Cost of Deals) profit x 100

**2. Net profit periphery:** Net profit periphery is a profitability statistic that calculates the proportion of deals and other income remaining after abating all company expenditures, similar as costs of products vending, operating charges, interest, and levies. Net profit periphery varies from gross profit periphery as a measure of overall business profitability, since it includes not just the cost of products vended but also all other connected expenditures.

Net Profit periphery = Net Profit/ profit * 100.

**3. Working capital:** Working capital measures a company's available operating liquidity, which may be employed to support day- to- day operations. Working capital equals current means minus current arrears.

**4. Debt/ Equity rate:** The debt- to- equity rate is a solvency statistic that indicates how much an establishment funds itself through equity vs debt. This rate gives insight into the company's solvency by indicating shareholder equity's capacity to cover all debt in the case of a business collapse.

Debt to Equity rate = Total Debt/ Total Equity

**5) Seasonality:** Seasonality is a measure of how the time of time influences your company's fiscal data and results.However, this metric can help you filter through the variations and view the numbers for what they are, If you work in an assiduity that's told by high and low seasons. It's vital to note that there are no absolute good or poor fiscal KPIs. Metrics should be compared to former times or assiduity challengers to determine if your company's fiscal performance is adding or falling, as well as how it compares to others.

## Common Pitfalls and Success Tips

My acquaintance started a business several times before. He was an intelligent, hardworking man who occasionally got lucky. His firm expanded steadily.

He also signed the contract that every aspiring company owner wishes for: one that will more than triple his revenues. Nothing compares to well-earned achievement, therefore he threw a wonderful party. He gave assignments to every employee, supplier, and dealer he could think of. After all, typical commercial thinking encourages us to celebrate our successes.

Or not. According to studies published in the journal Emotion, people regard "suggestive" victors — individuals who intimately and vocally enjoy their triumphs — less positively than "impassive" (read "humble") winners. It was thought that the noisy winners were less emotionally developed, egotistical, and unsuitable as musketeers. This is vital in business because, let's be honest, who wants to do business with someone who is so prideful and emotionally unsophisticated that they wouldn't make good musketeers?

"Suggestive winning" is only one of the effects of achieving a certain level of corporate success. Do you want to continue adding accomplishments to your list? Make an effort to prevent these repeated frequent issues.

## 1. An excessive level of confidence.

Confident people have less anxiety and fear. It removes emotional barriers, allowing you to serve more effectively under pressure. Until it isn't, it may be the coolest performance-enhancing drug ever.

According to a research published in the Journal of Personality and Social Psychology, early accomplishments increased a person's skill exposure to their task. Compared to the other two groups, (actors) overstated their once palms and anticipated future success. Participation increased prospects for future achievement and improved their appraisal of recent performance."

This is especially true if those early triumphs were primarily due to luck rather than competence. Though it cannot predict the future, the past may inform it. Pretenses are supplemented on a daily basis but are not compensated.

What is the optimal level of assurance? a confidence that stems from previous triumphs and confirms that you have the knowledge, skills, and moxie to make the proper decision, offer a successful product, and recruit the right labor force. You'll get the capacity to be precise with time and difficulties. Otherwise, do not presume that you were previously correct.

## 2. Throwing money at difficulties.

I know many successful entrepreneurs who did not
start from nothing. They had a dream, a vision, an idea. Nonetheless, they demanded any plutocrat. When presented with a difficulty, they approach it creatively and carefully. What about the initial challenges? They developed consistency and tenacity, which culminated in the assumption that intelligence, inventiveness, and rigidity are the fashionable methods to problem solving. Not cash.

However, if you are going to miss a delivery deadline, it may be tempting to invest more money for a speedier payload. The appeal of just hiring someone to handle your force control issues is considerable. Spending more plutocrats on stockpiles is more appealing than simplifying products to achieve just-in-time delivery.

Nonetheless, the structure for running a profitable business, no matter how large or little, is really basic. Profitable businesses generate more money than they spend. Clinging to the formula improves your chances of success. You're more likely to spend less than you earn if you can come up with a creative solution that costs nothing or a minuscule amount of money. Keep your expenses below your revenue.

### 3. A declining standard.
Initially, the stakes appear to be rather high. Each trade call looks to be critical to the outcome. You organize, schedule, and confirm. You go to any length to meet your obligations.

Success may eventually cause some of these norms to crumble. Is there one delivery date missing from the list of fifty? It is not very notable. chose not to spend the necessary time in medication and instead "sect" a product rally? You are going to be okay. Ignoring a difficult debate between two associates and failing to intervene? Everything will work itself out.

And before you realize it, the high standards you'd set for yourself and your employees have been supplanted by recommendations rather than authorization.
Culture is defined not just by what you support, but also by what you tolerate and allow to exist. Details you allow yourself and your employees to get down with. Consider the

specific stations and activities you support. Take extra time to evaluate the principles and behaviors that you can live with. Because, in the end, what you permit will decide the culture you wish to create, even if what you support may make it unique.

## How to prevent typical business mistakes.

### 1. Forming sensible financial ideas
Successful firms stick to a budget and avoid chasing phantom profits. Numerous firms want to take advantage of company owners. These scam artists make inflated promises to entice unsuspecting corporations to make quick decisions. But most of the time, they are simply leading you in the wrong way.Increasing productivity is something in which many firms participate. After all, plutocrats and time are synonymous.

However, in the days and weeks that follow, the maturity of organizations discovers that the operation is either utterly worthless or not worth learning how to utilize. That is a waste of plutocracy. Prudent spending is a defining characteristic of successful firms. They meticulously examine every expense, regardless of what is given, in order to compute the expected return on investment.

### 2. Always be prepared for calamities.
When people think of catastrophes, they tend to focus on the most disastrous ones. People identify catastrophes with occurrences such as fires, typhoons, earthquakes, and even booze-filled workplace parties. However, calamities happen in a variety of shapes and sizes. As people in Southern Australia can confirm, a blackout may be terrible for unprepared enterprises. An angry former employee taking a laptop is

likewise seen as a disaster. In fact, any unexpected incident that affects business might be considered a disaster.

A successful firm has a strategy in place to deal with any calamity, regardless of its magnitude or breadth. This guarantees that the event's negative impact is minimal. Not preparing for disasters is likely the most serious error a company can make, since it results in downtime, wasted money, and dissatisfied customers.

**3. Always consider your internet reputation.**
Social networking has transformed the way businesses develop their reputations. The traditional assumption was that a satisfied customer would tell a few people about their service, but a dissatisfied customer would tell 10 people.

Successful firms avoid two typical pitfalls when it comes to their internet reputation. The first step is to entirely distance yourself from what others are saying about your organization online. The second error is to respond angrily to complaints or opposing ideas.

Finding a medium ground is essential for effectively controlling one's online reputation. Cultivate connections with internet users who enjoy your company, and engage with those who had a negative experience to see what can be done to fix the problem. This not only helps to keep current customers, but it also demonstrates to new clients that if something goes wrong, you are eager to solve it.

## How to Make Financial issues simpler

Financial planning is vital, but it is also known to be an unpleasant process. Many people find that dealing with scary life events, such as having children in college or nearing retirement age, causes a great deal of emotional or mental stress. Others may feel overwhelmed as they consider many potential scenarios, obstacles, and solutions.

Without a doubt, there are several smaller, easier money activities you may perform fast to assist improve your financial status to some extent. However, there is no alternative for a comprehensive, detailed financial strategy.

Inflation. It's just one word, but it can cause dread in the hearts—and budgets—of customers. This year has been difficult for all of us, and a typical question we receive is, "How can I make my money go further?"

This is a real concern, especially as the gift-giving season approaches. There are several minor strategies to reduce your spending, such as cutting back on needless costs (which may include halting your morning coffee run for a time), buying for the holidays sooner than usual, and, of course, keeping an eye out for deals.

This year, numerous large box companies have already announced pre-Black Friday specials, and more are set to follow. Keep up to date by following your favorite businesses and brands on social media—you could find a fantastic deal on Christmas presents!
These money-saving strategies may seem insignificant—remember, they all add up!—but it can be tough to have the guts to examine our finances and commit to making larger adjustments.A smart beginning step is to allow yourself permission to spend 15-30 minutes per week working on your budget.

**Here are some financial principles, in no particular sequence, for you to consider.**

**1. Protect your funds from inflation:** High inflation rates affect more than simply basics such as petrol and food. They can also reduce your savings. Consider adopting techniques to offset losses, such as diversifying your financial portfolio, developing skills for a side business, or pursuing a promotion or raise to stay up with expenditures.

**2. Get ready for higher interest rates:** When interest rates are raised by the US Federal Reserve, what can you do to save? If your mortgage has a variable rate, you want to think about refinancing. This will assist prevent future hikes or decreases and lock in your payment at the existing low rates. Still, if you intend to embrace plutocrats, act incontinently before interest rates become too high.

Higher interest rates may result in greater returns on instrument and savings accounts. Gain more by learning how to apply a laddering method.

**3. Create a new spending plan:** Naturally, no amount of planning can fully prepare you for every potential expense. Considerations include vacation time, birthdays, expenses related to attending an academy, special occasions, and fluctuations in income throughout the year.

**4. Prepare for the impending significant event in your life:** What are you planning to watch? union? How about a house move? Retirement? Whatever it is, research the effects of this shift on your plutocrat. For those who are getting married? Spend some time discussing your financial goals, debts, and budgeting strategy with your spouse when you sit down to chat. In order to pay your expenses, you could also choose to use a connubial agreement. Having a kid? It's time to review your paid family leave benefits, investigate childcare options and costs, and create council savings accounts.

**5. Increase your retirement savings:** Should you not have already, start saving for retirement right now. If you're currently saving, think about increasing it by 1%. Little increases of this type can eventually add up to significant benefits without going against your current budget.

**6. Apply what you have learned from previous experiences:** Planning for the future frequently involves thinking back on the past. Analyze your spending and saving habits for the previous year to get understanding of possible changes for the next one. After surviving the difficulties presented by the pandemic, you might decide, for example, that you want to increase your emergency fund or diversify your investments in the case that a similar disaster happens.

**7. Raise the sum in your emergency fund:** Extra cash in your savings or bank account should not be used as an emergency fund. Make sure the account you create for this reason is flexible—that is, free from limitations that may lead to fines if used early. Emphasize accumulating an emergency reserve big enough to last for up to six months. Should you have started contributing to an emergency fund already, think about increasing the amount by a few dollars each pay period to help you get there sooner.

**8. Seek toward money accumulation:** To develop money, one needs time and planning. Invest, and keep it there. Steer clear of trading on and off the stock market every time it drops. Never leave money on the table with regard to the

401(k) plan that your company offers. To maximize your free money, make sure you contribute enough if you get matching funds! Borrow carefully, and keep an eye on your accounts frequently.

# CHAPTER 2: Setting Financial Goals

Establishing short-, medium-, and long-term financial goals is essential to achieving financial stability. You are more likely to spend more than is required if you aren't working toward a specific objective. Then, when you wish to retire, let alone when you need money for unanticipated bills, you won't have enough. You might end up in a vicious cycle of credit card debt and think you'll never have enough money for complete insurance, which makes you more vulnerable than you should be to cope with some of the major risks in life.

As the world learned during the pandemic and as many families continue to realize each month, no one is completely safe from disasters. You may sift through possible outcomes and try your best to prepare for them when you plan ahead. This should be an ongoing process so that you can adjust your goals and way of life to the inevitable changes that will come.

Establishing corporate financial goals can help businesses become more efficient and improve overall performance. Establishing appropriate financial goals might aid companies in effectively controlling expenses and tracking their advancement. Setting the right financial goals is essential if you are in control of an organization's finances.

Every dollar counts for small businesses. Making enough money to pay for ongoing operations is not enough; you also need to make plans for future growth.

Establishing financial goals enables you to concentrate on the larger picture while organizing the steps required to reach your goals. Financial objectives for a company may include saving up enough cash for new equipment or moving to a new satellite office. Here is how to begin, whatever they mean to you.

**Why are financial objectives important for businesses?**

Financial goal setting is a vital component of every small business plan. Whether you focus on numerical benchmarks or the physical acquisition of property, these goals serve as a road map to keep your organization on track for expansion.

Businesses may ensure that they are following a successful plan by establishing sales, cash flow, and other financial metrics goals and making modifications as needed.

**Examples of Financial Goals for Businesses**
To start setting more successful targets, you must first determine which areas need to be addressed. Here are some frequent examples of financial objectives for a business:

**1. Increase revenue.**
The primary goal of any small business is to raise profits and revenue. Improving profitability entails producing more revenue than you spend on business expenses. Revenue can be generated from a variety of sources, including interest on investments and sales.

**2. Increase margins.**

Another way to consider profit while setting financial goals is to look at your company's profit margin. This is the proportion of revenue that surpasses operating expenses. A corporation might set a profit margin objective that exceeds the industry standard. Assume your industry's typical profit margin is between 4% and 7%. Your company's profit margin is now 4.5%, so you might set a goal to increase it to the higher end of the industry standard.

## Goal-setting approaches for businesses

Once you've selected a few potential targets, you may put some tried-and-true strategies into action. One popular way is to set SMART goals. SMART is an acronym for "specific, measurable, attainable, realistic, and timely." In summary, you may use these elements to determine whether your financial goal is worth pursuing.

For example, you may want to earn more money. However, "earn more money" does not meet the SMART goal setting criteria since it lacks specifics. You might clarify your goal by stating how your organization will earn more money inside a certain timeframe. For example, you may change "earn more money" to "double sales in the next quarter by launching a new social media marketing campaign." This gives you a particular, tangible goal to pursue.

Whether you use SMART goal setting or not, all financial targets should be based on your current facts. Sit down and go over your company's financial statements, which comprise the cash flow statement, income statement, and balance sheet. This will provide you a clear view of your company's cash inflows and outflows, profit margins, and sales.

## How to Track Your Progress.

Smarter financial goal planning does not stop once you've defined your objectives and plan of action. It's also critical to monitor your progress along the way. Document all actions taken to implement the strategy, identifying each activity and its outcome. If you're saving for a specific goal, store the money in a separate account. Select the most important metrics to watch, such as total revenue, profit margins, or sales per quarter. You may follow these indicators over time to see how close you are to your objective.

Finally, keep in mind that no organization can fulfill all of its objectives. Analyze the methods used to find what worked best and adjust your approach to get greater results with future goals.

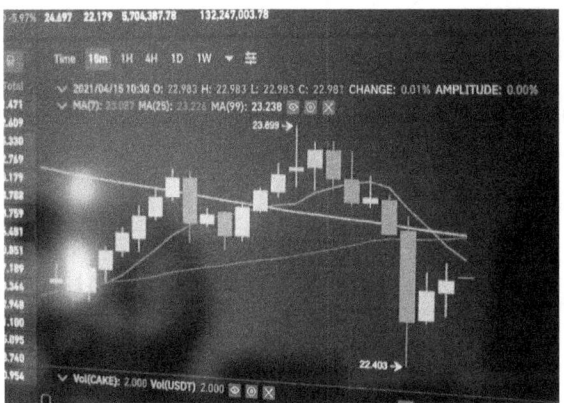

## Establishing Your Financial Goals

The carefully thought out and articulated financial vision will be respected and serve as a guide for your financial destiny. Selecting a financial route with you also aids in self-discovery and helps you identify your values.

At the beginning of the year, it's a good idea to revisit our concept of financial success. I often see in my seminars that students' conceptions of prosperity are far from uniform. Some individuals define success in terms of money: "I make $100,000 a year, so I'm successful." Some people consider it to be their way of life: "My $70,000 sports car makes me successful." Conversely, some individuals associate their success in life with their net worth, stating statements such as "My net worth of approximately one million dollars makes me successful."

These definitions state that the objective is to become financially successful. I have a totally different idea of what financial success is. I believe that achieving financial success is a process.

To put it simply, I believe that the degree of our financial success is based on how successfully we achieve our financial goals.

When I talk about financial goals, I'm not talking about the big, long-term ones like buying a house or retiring. These are essential. Setting short-term goals, however, is the best way to accomplish our goals and keep ourselves motivated to live within (or below) our means.

If our main financial ambitions are ones that need years or decades of saving and hundreds or millions of dollars, it will be very impossible for us to stay motivated to fulfill such goals. Why? We just don't associate large amounts of money meant for uses that won't occur for ten or twenty years with our everyday activities—and, more importantly, our daily expenditures.

However, if our financial goals are modest and immediate (less than a year away and less than $1,000), we might be able to understand their scope and timing more easily and let them influence our daily decisions in a constructive way.

For the sake of argument, let's say that one day I am enjoying some soup that I brought to work (this occurs a lot). After a while, I might start to consider going out to lunch instead. In the end, "It's only an additional ten dollars to relax a little and dine at a nice sit-down restaurant! That ten dollars won't really hinder me from earning a million dollars when I retire, right? Well, it isn't accurate. It will. Ten dollars a day for thirty years comes to $108,000. But if you invest the same ten dollars a day for thirty years at an average return of nine percent, you'll have more than half a million dollars. Enjoy the next thirty years of eating out every day. Make sure you order a beer to help you feel better about losing out on potential interest earnings of $440,000.

But in five months, when I want to spend $500 on a weekend trip to a mountain lodge with my partner, I'll quickly realize that every extra ten dollars I spend on eating out will go a long way toward achieving my goal. Well, two percent! And since I'm an expert in math, it would only take me the remainder of the morning to figure out that I would need to cut out fifty more meals from restaurants (for a two-month period) in order to equalize my savings to the full amount of my aim.

Thus, setting our own financial objectives is the key to achieving financial success. If you want to set significant, long-term goals, let's go ahead and do that. All we need to do is break them up into monthly objectives, if not weekly or even daily ones.

Wendy, my wife, is a prime illustration of this. Back in 2009, she and I had discussed our desire to take our small family on a week-long Disney cruise. Disregarding the argument about whether a Disney cruise, or any cruise, is a wise choice for a family with a one-year-old who isn't potty trained and a three-year-old, let me tell you what that talk did for us. We finally made up our minds to take our family on a cruise in the fall of 2010. Once we set that goal, my spouse spent the following year researching the costs of hotels, airfare, cruise tickets, and even a few days of theme park entry in Orlando. She was continually looking for sales and was effective in doing so since we had decided on and highlighted that goal in our calendars. Over the course of the next year, she also found bargains on inexpensive accommodation and travel, which reduced the whole budget for those goods to a small fraction of what was originally planned.

Wendy and I were able to cajole her mother and her closest friend into joining us after converting our "someday wish" into a goal by putting it on paper, going over it often, and having conversations about it. Consequently, we enjoyed an amazing two weeks together, laughed a lot, overindulged in food (as cruisers like to do), handled a few meltdowns, created some amazing memories, and only suffered one family member's fracture.

Unspoken objectives continue to be unmet desires.

Detailed Financial Objectives

Setting clear, uncomplicated financial objectives and recording them in paper are essential.

Setting up one or three financial objectives is a smart first step.

• Talk about and list all the things you want to buy or do that will cost you no more than $1,000.

• Choose the month and year you wish to finish or reach your objective. Don't just enter "in six months," as this will appear every time you see your objective. Put the year and the month in writing, being precise.

• Calculate the total amount of money you will need to save to accomplish this objective. Calculate the monthly equivalent of that amount.

Lastly, if you are with a partner, remember to include them in these procedures. While it may not ensure a flawless relationship, having shared and mutually acceptable financial objectives is, in my opinion, the greatest way to reduce money-related fights.

## How to Define Your Financial Vision: What You Should and Should Not Do

1. You need more than just desires to keep you going.

2. Avoid pursuing wealth for its own sake. If not, your "wishes" for wealth are merely motivated by avarice.

3. Avoid having financial arguments with your spouse. Instead of seeing money as a sign of incompatibility, make use of it as inspiration to create shared objectives that make money your ally rather than your enemy.

4. Do jot down a clear objective on a few little pieces of paper, around the size of a business card.

5. Hang a goal card on your bathroom mirror, nightstand or refrigerator.

6. Keep a goal card in your wallet or purse mixed in with your credit or debit cards so that every time you make a transaction, you are compelled to check your objectives.

7. Do read your objectives aloud and discuss them at least once a day.

8. If you have deep relationships with spouses, parents, siblings, kids, closest friends, and so on, do think about expressing your objectives with them. They can support us as we go.

## How to Measure Progress with Precision

Measurement of your success is essential for several reasons. First of all, by showing you how much work still has to be done, it keeps you inspired and concentrated on your goals. Second, it lets you adapt your strategies and tactics in case you run across difficulties or roadblocks or if your situation changes. Thirdly, it helps you to recognize your accomplishments and give yourself something for them, which boosts your self-esteem and contentment.

There are several ways to gauge progress depending on the goal. Typical quantitative methods of monitoring results are numbers, percentages, and other units of measurement. By use of comments, views, or observations, qualitative methods examine performance. Visual approaches convey data and patterns via graphs, charts, and other visual aids. If your target weight is ten pounds in three months, for instance, you may track your progress by regularly weighing yourself and figuring out how much weight you've dropped or still need to lose. Should you want to enhance your public speaking skills, you may gauge your progress by asking for audience comments or by filming and reviewing your recordings. Build a savings tracker that shows how much money you have saved each month and how close you are to reaching your goal if your aim is to save $5,000 over the course of a year.

# How to Track Your Development

Having both personal and professional objectives might help you feel more successful and productive, particularly if the goal is significant to you. A good goal must include measuring your progress as it enables you to rank your activities and project how long it will take to complete each one. Tracking your development can also let you choose how to modify your strategy, which will accelerate your development.This article will discuss the need of tracking progress, how to evaluate your personal development, and practical applications of progress assessment.

## Why should progress be tracked?

Setting a goal and then monitoring your advancement might help you achieve it. It can help you determine which methods work best and what sort of behaviors support your development. Then you may include these strategies into your overall strategy for accomplishing a certain objective. Monitoring your development might also reveal how near you are to reaching your objective. You could be motivated to continue by this and be reminded of your objectives.

## Approaching Progress Measurement

To track your development successfully, think about the following actions:

### 1. Select your goals.
You have to identify what action and result you desire before you can create short- and long-term objectives. If you want to do this successfully, think about looking at how a part of your

company is now doing. Using that information, then, create a clear goal.On social media, for instance, a business may aim for a million followers and discover that it now has 200,000. The marketing department of the organization may then set precise short- and long-term goals for gaining 800,000 followers, including launching an advertising campaign aimed at potential followers.

## 2. Give yourself a deadline.

By giving yourself a deadline to reach long-term objectives, you may improve how you handle finishing short-term tasks. Think about putting your approach on paper along with the amount of time you intend to spend on each step. As you prepare, take into account going over the processes to foresee any issues and provide solutions. This can help you become more adept at managing your time, which can facilitate meeting deadlines.Tracking the time and method you finish a job can also help you create a timeline. This enables you to assess and enhance your methods for finishing tasks, which will support your long-term goals. A publishing house would, for instance, demand a writer to complete a 100,000-word book within two years of signing a deal. The writer can set short-term objectives, such as writing a certain amount of words per day, to track their progress toward their two-year target.

## How to Assess Advancement

To successfully track your development, consider the following actions:

## 1. Determine what you want to accomplish.

Before you can create long-term and short-term goals, you must first choose the type of activity and outcome you wish to achieve. To accomplish this successfully, consider examining the existing state of an area inside your firm that you wish to improve. Create a specific objective based on your newfound understanding.For example, a company may set a goal of having one million social media followers but only have 200,000 right now. The organization's marketing staff may then set specific short- and long-term goals to acquire 800,000 followers, such as launching an advertisement campaign aimed at potential followers.

## 2. Set a due date.
Set timelines for long-term goals to make it easier to accomplish short-term activities. Consider defining each phase of your approach in writing, including how long you want to spend on each. When establishing plans, consider evaluating the procedures to foresee difficulties and come up with solutions. This can help you improve your time management and meet deadlines more easily.Another technique to create a timeline is to record when and how you finish activities. This can help you achieve your long-term goals by allowing you to assess and improve your work completion strategies. For example, if a writer and a publishing business agree on a 100,000-word book, the corporation may require the writer to complete the work within two years. To track their progress toward their two-year objective, the writer may set short-term targets, such as the number of words they write each day.

## 3. Establish benchmarks.
A milestone is a little accomplishment that may be used to track your progress towards a larger goal. Milestones may improve your ability to concentrate by allowing you to visualize each stage of your strategy and providing you with a sense of success upon completion. Consider defining a small goal, such as completing a task by a specified day or

time.Completing all of a college student's curriculum each semester might be a significant accomplishment if the student plans to teach marine biology. This allows them to track their progress toward their long-term professional objective and estimate the time necessary to complete it.

**4. Transform your goals into smart ones.**
Sensible objectives are time constrained, purposeful, quantifiable, attainable, and explicit. Setting realistic goals allows you to track your progress by:

• **Assigning specific tasks to monitor:** Clearly articulating your objectives and breaking them down into achievable phases might assist you understand the processes needed to achieve long-term goals. This may also help you estimate how long it will take to achieve your goals in an acceptable manner.

• **Determine whether your goals can be measured:** Use time as a metric to guarantee that your target is quantifiable. This may be accomplished by creating a timetable that will help you determine the number of activities to do, the amount of time required for each activity, and the overall amount of time required to attain your objective.

• **Making your objectives attainable:** Setting long-term goals and employing milestones might help you guarantee that your goals are achievable because certain jobs get simpler to do with time. Assessing the reality of your objectives may also help you determine whether you need to learn any extra skills. Following that, you may keep track of your progress by noting the skills you've acquired and the successes of your goals.

• **Evaluate the relevance of your objectives:** Before setting goals, it is vital to confirm that they are appropriate. This may help you revise, update, or rewrite your objectives to ensure they still satisfy your requirements. This can also enhance your time management abilities, making it easy to track your progress.

• **Developing time-sensitive action plans:** Making a timeline allows you to easily see how far you've come toward a specific goal, which may help you track your progress. This may help you create reasonable timescales and alter unrealistic ones.

### 5. Monitor and assess development.

Recording progress is a realistic way to measure it. Consider setting out your major goals, assignments, due dates, and milestones. Next, you may track your progress by marking tasks as you complete them and accomplishments as you achieve them on a calendar or planner. You may use the information in your planner to choose whether to add a new assignment or change your schedule.If a test-taker wants to pass a certification exam with a good score, they can utilize a calendar to schedule the test and set a study deadline. To help students stay focused on their long-term objective, they might identify the subjects they need to master, estimate how much time they will spend studying each day, and create milestones.

# CHAPTER 3: Budgeting by the Numbers

Use the 50/30/20 budget to make the most of your money. You use around half of your pre-tax income on necessities, such as making the minimum payments on your debts. At least 20% goes toward savings and extra debt payments beyond the minimum, and no more than 30% is allocated to wants.

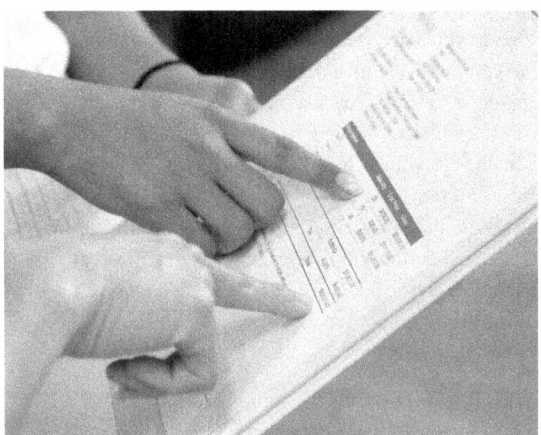

**This straightforward method will assist you in developing a reasonable budget that you can adhere to over time in order to meet your financial goals.**

### 50%: Requirements

Needs are the things you need to survive and the bills you have to pay. These obligations and demands should be covered by half of your after-tax income. You will need to either reduce your wants or try to downsize your lifestyle, such as going to a smaller home or driving a smaller car, if you spend more money on needs than that. Cooking more often at home, carpooling, or using public transportation to work are all possible options. Instances of "needs" consist of, but are not restricted to:

• Minimum debt payments; • Rent or mortgage; • Car payments; • Groceries; • Health care and insurance; • Utility bills

### Of them, thirty percent are wishes.

Everything you buy that isn't absolutely necessary is a desire. When it comes straight down, everything in the "wants" category is optional. You may cook instead of going out to dine, work out at home instead of going to the gym, or watch sports on TV instead of buying tickets.

This section addresses upgrades, including selecting between paying for cable TV and watching television for free with an antenna, or between buying a Mercedes over a more affordable Honda. All of the little items you purchase to bring joy and excitement into your life are essentially wishes. The following are only a few instances of "wants":

Extraneous apparel and accessories, including
- bags or jewelry.
- Tickets for sporting activities.
- Vacations taken for leisure or non-essential reasons.
- The most current technology (especially a development over a fully working model that came before it).
- Streaming via a very fast Internet.

**20% is reimbursed.**
At list, try to set aside and invest twenty percent of your net income. It is advised that you keep emergency reserves of at least three months in case you lose your job or encounter other unforeseen circumstances. Focus then on reaching your long-term financial goals and retirement. Example of savings might be:
Setting up an emergency fund.
Contributing IRA money to mutual fund accounts. Stock purchases.

• Paying back more than the bare minimum due. • Setting aside funds to buy a house over the long haul.

## The Value of Savings
The United States has an exceptionally large debt load, yet Americans are infamously bad savers. The average personal savings rate in the United States was just 3.7% in December 2023.

The purpose of the 50-30-20 rule is to help people manage their after-tax income so they can save money for retirement and emergencies. Establishing an emergency fund has to be a top priority for every household in case of unanticipated medical expenses, job loss, or other financial obligations.

Replacing an emergency fund should be the household's top priority if it is used.

The importance of retirement savings increases as individuals live longer. A satisfying retirement may be ensured by estimating your retirement needs, setting a goal early, and working toward it.

### The 50/30/20 Budget Rule's benefits

In several ways, the 50/30/20 rule may assist people in becoming financially wealthy. Potential advantages of following these suggestions include:

**1. Usability:** The 50/30/20 rule makes budgeting simple to comprehend and implement by offering a clear structure. You don't need to do intricate calculations in order to swiftly distribute your earnings. These guidelines are simple enough for even the least financial literate person to understand.

**2. Setting crucial expenditures in order of importance:** By setting these costs in order of importance, you can make sure that you can satisfy your basic needs without going over budget or taking on excessive debt. This plan makes sure that your necessities are taken care of because these requirements state that half of your income must go toward necessities.

**3. Long-term financial stability:** By adhering to these recommendations, you regularly set away 20% of your income as savings for your future financial security. This savings expenditure might contribute to your long-term financial objectives, help you accumulate wealth, and provide you and your family a sense of security as you near retirement.

**Implementing the 50/30/20 Budget Rule**

Keeping to a budget requires no one, universal method. These are some generally beneficial fundamental ideas for creating a 50/30/20 budget.

**1. Track Your Spending**

You may learn your spending patterns better by keeping track of your expenses for a few months. Sort your expenditure according to the 50/30/20 rule by allocating it among savings, desires, and necessities. This will enable you to visualize how much over budget you will be right immediately. Moreover, the only way to be positive you are remaining under your budget is to monitor your actual expenditure. Usually, this is made simple with spreadsheet programs like Microsoft Excel.

**2. Identify your income.**

You determine the 50/30/20 budget by looking at your revenue. Recognize that your gross income may vary much from your net profits since federal income taxes reduce your take-home pay. Knowing your actual income and the amount that enters your bank account each pay period may make it simpler to set up the appropriate budget figures for the three categories.

**3. Decide which costs are essential.**

This includes the cost of food, fuel, rent or mortgage payments, energy, insurance, and debt repayment. Since you need these fees for daily existence, they are unavoidable. These expenses need to be given top priority since they could eat up most of your money. When you acquiesce to these costs, you also have the least number of options because they have to be paid.

**4. Establish a savings account that operates automatically.**

Cost reductions will result from the automated approach. Using your checking account, set up automatic monthly transfers to your investment or savings accounts. This guarantees a consistent increase of your money without requiring physical labor. Your savings could not be as administratively heavy, which would let you often review your budget to make sure it still corresponds with your expenditures and financial objectives.

### 5. Keep up the consistency.

The 50/30/20 fiscal concepts need consistency. Refuse to go over budget or alter your % allocation and instead adhere to your spending plan. Like any other budget, this one functions best when its parameters are made very clear and routinely used. Strive for consistency from one month to the next and take care to modify your monthly expenditure limits.

## Example of the 50/30/20 budget rule.

Imagine Elaine is a lady who recently graduated from college and began her first full-time job. She wants to establish excellent money habits from the start and has heard of the 50/30/20 budget guideline. She chooses to create a 50/30/20 budget in order to gain control of her financial situation.

To better understand her spending habits, Elaine begins documenting her costs for a month. She utilizes a budgeting tool that automatically categorizes her spending as needs, desires, and savings. She also estimates her monthly after-tax income, which is $3,500. This will be her starting point for distributing her funds using the 50/30/20 guideline.

After reviewing her monitored spending, Elaine discovers that her necessary expenses, such as rent, utilities, groceries, transportation, and student loan payments, total around $1,750 per month. She devotes exactly 50% of her salary, $1,750, to meeting these demands. She then devotes $1,050 to discretionary expenses and $700 a month to retirement and savings. And she arranges for an automated transfer from her checking account to her savings account on payday.

Six months later, Elaine gets a promotion. Because her income has changed, she reevaluates each budget amount, checks her total budget, and makes adjustments as appropriate. She also learns that her transportation expenditures are more than intended, so she chooses to start carpooling with a coworker to save money.

Elaine maintains discipline and consistency in her budgeting practices. She emphasizes her financial well-being and periodically assesses her progress toward her objectives. As her career grows, she makes adjustments to her budget to reflect changes in her income and priorities. She has taken precautions to ensure that not only her current requirements are covered, but that she also has enough money saved for the future.

## Reasons to Create a Savings Strategy.

Prolonged Safety Because the future is unpredictable, financial troubles might develop at any time. By saving money, you may develop a safety net for unexpected costs and future purchases. You feel safer the more you save because you are better prepared to face anything life throws at you.

**Saving money requires self-control and sacrifice.**

Many Americans are falling behind on their retirement savings, while others are not saving at all, according to a Bankrate survey.

It is unusual to argue against the benefits of saving money. One of the most important (and frequently offered) pieces of financial advice is to save. Even though saving money is crucial, many of us don't do it. Understanding that you should save money is insufficient for making sound financial decisions.

This also makes sense. You cannot consistently achieve anything until you understand why you are working so hard and saving money in the first place. After all, saving money requires self-control and some level of giving up.

Long-term success of your savings plan hinges on your knowledge of its advantages. Should you want aid in appreciating the significance of saving money, take into consideration the following main justifications in favor of beginning immediately:

**1. You may save your way to liberty.**

If you have no particular purpose in mind, it could be tough to set aside money for a savings account. When what you want can be gotten today, why save for later? You'll surely discover something eventually that you want to save for, even if you're not sure what you're saving for right now. This is merely one of the several incentives for retaining money. You have choices whether buying your child a new house, car, or school. Setaway money is also vital for unanticipated bills and emergencies.

"It has nothing to do with money, and everything to do with giving yourself freedom and choice in your life," explains Eric Roberge, CFP®, the founder of a financial planning service that aids individuals in their 30s in handling their money.

"When you have money available in the bank you can do what you want without stress," he adds. If you're confused about the necessity of conserving money, consider enabling yourself to do as you wish rather than feeling forced to work for a particular corporation or in a certain region because of your compensation.

To what degree you should save may differ depending on your financial goals. Maybe you have a certain purpose in mind, such as traveling and leaving your work for a year. When you elect not to work during this period, you should calculate out how much money you will need to pay both your holiday and your daily living needs.

Should obtaining flexibility be one of your savings aims, you may set aside a particular number each month (a hint: automate your saves).
Set up your savings account as a "build wealth fund," says Roberge. Saving money in this scenario signifies having money accessible to you anytime and anything you choose.

## 2. Stability in finances may be achieved by saving.

"I love saving money because it means having financial security," says Kara Perez, the creator of a nonprofit organization devoted to financial education, whose goal is to empower women by providing them with the information and tools they need to reach their financial goals.

According to Perez, "money, in a word, eases life." "I save because I don't want to get caught in a financial emergency and I want my future self to enjoy the same wonderful lifestyle I do now."

Perez advises putting money down in a brokerage account where you may make investments for the future as well as a liquid savings account where you can keep cash on hand for unforeseen expenses and emergencies.

**3. Saving allows you to take reasonable risks.**

Saving money is important in order to establish financial reserves, which allow you to take measured chances with less stress. If you don't have any funds, it may be difficult to follow some interests. Consider launching a business, for instance. To start a small firm, you will need financial support.

However, if you create a savings goal and contribute to it each month, you may pursue new chances, even if they have a temporary impact on your wages (if you start as a small company owner, paychecks may be delayed to arrive at first).

## Why Should You Save Money?

The value of saving money is straightforward: it helps you to have more stability in your life. If you have funds set away for emergencies, you have a backup plan in case anything unexpected happens. Furthermore, if you have cash set up for discretionary spending, you may be able to take chances or try something new. There are plenty of good reasons to save money, right?

If you're sure that you should save money, start saving by creating an online savings account. And the good news is that becoming a saver does not need a complete lifestyle shift. There are easy strategies to save money that you may start doing immediately. Once you've developed the practice of saving, you'll forget when you didn't.

**Six Simple Ways to Reduce Costs**

Having a strategy makes saving simpler, so follow these steps. Beginning to save money may be the most difficult task. This rigorous process will help you build a clear and practical strategy for saving for all of your short- and long-term objectives.

**1. Keep track of your spending:** Understanding how much you spend is the first step in saving money. Make a list of everything you spend money on, including coffee, home items, cash tips, and monthly expenses. You may record your costs using whichever method works best for you, such as pen and paper, a basic spreadsheet, or a free online spending tracker or app. After gathering your data, organize it into categories such as food, mortgage, and petrol, and then tally up the totals. Check your bank and credit card statements to be sure you've included everything.

**2. Incorporate saving into your budget:** Now that you've identified your monthly spending, you can start creating a budget. To help you regulate your spending and avoid overspending, your budget should show you how your costs and income are related. Budget for costs like automobile maintenance, which occur often but not every month. Make sure your budget contains a savings area, and attempt to save as much as you are initially comfortable with. Eventually, you should save 15-20% of your paycheck.

3. **Look for methods to minimize costs:** If your savings aren't meeting your objectives, it may be time to reduce your spending. Determine which expenses are not absolutely required, such as dining out and entertainment. Look for methods to save money on set monthly bills like mobile phone subscriptions and car insurance. Additional techniques to reduce everyday spending include:

Examine your recurrent costs and remove any memberships or subscriptions that you no longer use, particularly if they renew automatically.

Consider the expense of cooking at home versus going out: Make it a habit to eat the majority of your meals at home. When you do want to splurge, look into the specials at neighboring eateries.

If you're tempted to acquire something non-essential, fight the desire and wait a few days. If it turns out that the item was more of a want than a requirement, you might devise a strategy to save money for it.

**4. Having a goal is one of the best ways to save money:** Think initially on your savings goals for the near term (one to three years) and long term (four or more years). Find out then how much money has to be saved and how long it will take.

**5. Automate your savings:** Almost all banks let you to program automatic transfers from your checking to savings accounts. You get to decide which direct deposit accounts get a portion of your paychecks directly into your savings account as well as how much, when, and where the money is transferred. The advantage is that you won't be under any stress over it and will thus be less likely to overspend. Spare change programs and credit card rewards are two other easy methods to save money. The former rounds purchases to the closest dollar and puts the difference into a savings or investing account.

**6. Track your progress by looking at your monthly spending plan:** This will enable you to identify and deal with problems fast and keep you on track with your personal savings target. Gaining knowledge of money management techniques may even inspire you to come up with new ways to save and advance.

## How to Adjust Your Budget for Maximum Efficiency

Setting up and maintaining a marketing budget is more than simply a good idea in today's company climate. It's a crucial aspect of ensuring your brand's long-term success. Here's all you need to know about managing a marketing budget to succeed.

Every organization, regardless of sector, specialization, or long-term aspirations, must have a good marketing budget. A marketing budget not only helps a company correctly plan its advertising approach, but it also simplifies the process of calculating overall return on investment.

However, creating a marketing budget from the beginning (or making significant adjustments to a current one) might be difficult if you don't know where to begin. Here, we'll go over all you need to know about managing a marketing budget and preparing your firm for long-term success.

## How to Manage Marketing Budgets

Ready to begin the process of creating, executing, and monitoring a marketing budget that will provide results? Here are some key measures to do.

### 1. Choose between quarterly and yearly budgets.

Although many organizations establish and set their marketing budgets annually, quarterly budgeting is also typical. If you manage a small or new business, have a restricted budget, or are unfamiliar with marketing budgets, going quarterly may offer you a better opportunity of determining what works best for your company and goals.

### 2. Understand our target market.

Before you can pick which sorts of marketing to prioritize when allocating your marketing budget, you must first understand who you are marketing to. Creating a list of buyer personas might help you get inside your target audience's brains and design a more successful plan.

Begin the process of creating new buyer personas by interviewing both current customers and members of your target groups. Google Analytics and other tools can assist you in determining which demographics your current visitors fall into.

### 3. Decide on your marketing channels

Once you know where your potential clients go for information about items and services similar to yours, you'll be able to determine which marketing channels to focus on in the future. Examples include:

**Outbound marketing:** Outbound strategies are effective for disseminating your brand's message to a large portion of your target audience. TV commercials, display advertisements, and cold email outreach are some examples.

Inbound marketing: Inbound strategies allow you to engage with customers who are already interested in the things you provide or the themes your brand addresses. Examples include blog articles, ebooks, SEO material, and video marketing content.

Digital marketing includes fundamentals such as social media marketing, opt-in email marketing, content marketing, SEO, and PPC advertising.

**Brand-building:** This category focuses on achieving goals such as increasing brand recognition and usually overlaps or combines with a company's digital marketing activities.

Based on what you know about your target demographic, determine the importance of each channel to your current marketing strategy. Then, explore several techniques for allocating your budget among them. Regularly evaluate your progress and make modifications as needed.

Many organizations choose for the 10%-of-revenue option, which we discussed before. However, you may also base your budget on how much your competitors are spending or on specific goals you are working toward at the time. You may also use a top-down strategy, allowing management to reassess the final results on a yearly or quarterly basis.

# Why You Should Monitor Your Marketing Expenses

When it comes to money, there is no such thing as being too cautious. It's possible to overpay more than you anticipate, especially on certain sorts of marketing costs.

Having a strategy in place guarantees that you aren't wasting money and that you're spending it wisely. Establishing an appropriate marketing budget includes:

• Eliminates guesswork in marketing campaign planning
• Streamlines financial tracking
 • Improves ROI tracking
• Motivates teams to improve strategies
• Quickly eliminates unprofitable approaches in favor of effective marketing tactics.

It goes without saying that making money costs money. However, without a marketing budget, it is hard to determine how much is too much to spend. (A decent rule of thumb is to allocate roughly 10% of your income to marketing.)

Setting and managing a marketing budget allows each organization to choose how much of its money should be allocated to different components of a marketing campaign, such as pay-per-click advertising vs content marketing.

## Tools for Marketing Budget Management:

In the digital era, there are numerous tools available to help you manage your marketing budget. Here are some possibilities worth considering:

**Proof:** This comprehensive product is an excellent choice for marketing managers looking for a single platform that can handle everything from analytics to budget-driven campaign planning.

**Uptempo:** Previously known as Allocadia, Uptempo is another excellent all-in-one tool for budget planners of all skill levels. Oversee finances, manage workflow, use predictive analytics, and more.

**Planful:** Planful is an excellent solution for simplifying the way your marketing department already prepares, finalizes, analyses, and reports, saving you time, effort, and money overall.
WriterAccess is a top-tier content creation platform that eliminates the guesswork from cost-effective, large-scale content development. Assemble a team of skilled writers and content producers to make your marketing material shine.

# CHAPTER 4: Advanced Financial Strategies

In today's fast-paced world, financial success entails more than simply conserving money. It necessitates a well-planned approach that extends beyond the fundamentals of budgeting and investing. Welcome to the realm of Advanced Financial Planning, where we dig into the finer points of managing your finances for a safe and wealthy future.

Advanced Financial Strategy is a complete approach to financial management that takes into account both your present status and your long-term ambitions. It entails examining many financial elements, making smart decisions, and being adaptable to changes in your life and the market.

**Importance of Advanced Financial Strategy**
Financial stability and prosperity are not accidents; they are the outcome of rigorous planning and execution. Here's why advanced financial strategy is important:

**1. Achieve your goals.**
Setting clear financial objectives and developing a plan to reach them improves your chances of fulfilling your aspirations, whether they be to purchase a home, send your children to college, or retire comfortably.

**2. Secure your future.**
Advanced Financial Strategy guarantees that you have a plan in place to cover unexpected bills, emergencies, and

retirement. It assists you in creating a nest egg that will provide you with financial security in your elderly years.

### 3. Reduce financial stress.
A well-structured financial plan allows you to confidently handle life's ups and downs. This relieves financial stress and allows you to focus on what is genuinely important to you.

### The Key Elements of Advanced Financial Planning
A successful Advanced Financial Strategy consists of several key components, each of which is crucial to your financial success. Let's look at them in detail:

### 1. Budget and Expense Tracking
Advanced Financial Planning begins with creating a precise budget and tracking your spending. It helps you understand where your money is going and allows you to make more educated spending decisions.

### 2. Debt Management.
Managing debt is critical for financial success. Learn how to manage and eliminate debt while increasing wealth.

### 3. Investment Strategy.
Explore the world of investing, which includes stocks, bonds, real estate, and more. Learn how to create a diverse portfolio that is aligned with your objectives and risk tolerance.

### 4. Retirement Planning.
Plan for retirement early to guarantee you have enough money to enjoy your senior years. Learn how to make the most of your retirement savings.

### 5. Tax optimization.

Investigate tax-efficient techniques to help you save money and improve your financial strategy.

### 6. Estate Planning.
Ensure that your assets are safe and dispersed in accordance with your intentions. Recognize the importance of estate planning, trusts, and wills.

### 7. Risk Management.
Understand the many forms of insurance and how they may protect you and your family from unforeseen catastrophes.

### What is the main purpose of advanced financial planning?
The primary purpose of Advanced Financial Strategy is to assist people and families in achieving financial security and success by establishing specific financial goals and developing a thorough strategy to attain them.

### How can Advanced Financial Strategy alleviate financial stress?
Advanced Financial Strategy lowers financial stress by giving an organized approach to financial management, establishing an emergency fund, and maintaining long-term financial stability.

### Is Advanced Financial Strategy just for the wealthy?
Advanced Financial Strategy is for everyone. It is a proactive approach to personal finance that may help people of all income levels.

### What are some frequent pitfalls to avoid in Advanced Financial Planning?
Common errors to avoid in Advanced Financial Strategy include failing to budget, not saving for retirement, and failing to diversify your investments.

**How frequently should I evaluate my Advanced Financial Plan?**
It is recommended that you evaluate your Advanced Financial Plan once a year or if there are substantial life events, such as marriage, childbirth, or a change in job.

**How can I locate a competent Advanced Financial Planner?**
To discover a certified Advanced Financial Planner, search for qualifications such as Certified Financial Planner (CFP) and seek referrals from reliable sources.

## How to Overcome Financial Fears and Misconceptions

Financial monsters come in all shapes and sizes. Some typical ones are running out of money, incurring high-interest debt, and constantly borrowing money. Making a strategy to address your financial concerns is the most effective method to conquer them.

**In this article:**

1. Running out of money
2. Dealing with high-interest debt
3. Constantly borrowing money

Chances are you have a few financial skeletons in your closet, and they might be plaguing you. That might generate a lot of stress and prevent you from enjoying the life you desire. There are many money-related fears out there, whether it feels like there's never enough money to go around or you're drowning in debt. Here are some of the more typical ones, as well as strategies for keeping your financial life from becoming a horror story.

## 1. Running out of money

According to a recent CNBC and Momentive study, almost 70% of Americans feel anxious about their money. Running out of money can be a significant financial concern, especially for those who live paycheck to paycheck.

**The following suggestions can help stop the cycle:**

• **Review your budget:** A budget is essentially a strategy for allocating your income and spending. If yours has to be rebooted, the 50/30/20 rule, zero-based budget, and 50/15/5 rule can all assist. Budgeting applications are another alternative. Budgeting, regardless of the approach you choose, may help keep your money under control.

• **Prepare for non-monthly costs:** Some bills are due at unusual periods of the year. Biannual insurance premiums and your child's summer camp cost are also ideal examples.

Planning for non-monthly costs might help you stick to your budget and avoid financial problems later on. To do so, divide the entire cost by 12 months and set away the required amount each month so that you may pay from savings when the expenditure arrives.

• **Keep track of how much you spend:** This can keep you responsible for your spending plan and help you identify hidden costs that are straining your budget. Set aside a few minutes each week for a brief money check-in. Use this opportunity to analyze your budget and make any necessary changes. If you split money with your partner, you may wish to include them in the talk.

### 2. Dealing with Debt at High Interest
High-interest debt is debt with an interest rate of 8% or more; if it is carried over month to month, it can erode wealth. The Federal Reserve notes that credit card average annual percentage rates (APRs) now surpass 21%. Debt cycle trapping is a fairly easy thing to achieve. Your credit and financial position can both benefit from breaking free.

**To get there, consider these suggestions:**

• **List all you owe:** Knowledge of your debt position is the first step. Note all of your account balances, interest rates, and minimum payments. Visit your creditors or connect into your online accounts to get this information.

• **Select a strategy of debt payback:** Several options exist to pay off debt. Whereas the debt avalanche technique concentrates on paying off your highest-interest debt first, the debt snowball approach stresses the account with the lowest amount. Using whatever strategy, you will pay as little as possible on your other accounts and as much as possible into the priority account. You shift the cash you were donating to that account to the next one on your list as you pay off each one.

• **Give consolidation of debt some thought:** A debt consolidation loan allows you to bundle many accounts into one payment. Then coming ahead, you will only have to make one monthly payment. You can eventually save money if the interest rate on your new loan is lower than it was on your prior ones. Moving high-interest debt to a balance transfer credit card with a 0% APR initially is an alternative option. These cards give up to 21 months interest-free bill payback. Just remember to pay off the balance before the intro period ends, failing which any outstanding debt will be charged the card's usual rate.

### 3. Continual requirement for borrowing money.
A financial shock could make your budget scream. Should you lack the requisite finances, you might have to take out extra debt or borrow from friends or family.

**Here are some strategies to keep away from it.**

• **Set up a significant emergency fund:** Try to accumulate three to six months of spending into a high-yield savings account. This can help you gain money on your assets and handle both major and minor financial challenges.

• **Create a savings-included budget:** Make a monthly savings goal that makes sense for you a regular line item in your budget. Short-term savings are allowed by both the 50/15/5 and 50/30/20 criteria.

• **Make savings automated:** You won't probably hit your objective overnight. Most crucial is to create the saving habit.

Establish recurring payments to your savings account to preserve regularity.

Owning a business may make money management tough. You may easily become buried in spreadsheets and data and start to doubt your ability to make sensible financial choices. You have to know your figures in order to manage a profitable firm.

Monitoring your expenditure and revenue allows you to make intelligent decisions based on financial facts and to better appreciate the status of your firm. Your capacity to spot possible concerns early on and act before they grow worse will come from money management.

It is time to set your anxieties aside and manage your money so you may build a prosperous firm.

Because there are so many unforeseen factors, especially with relation to money, running a business is tough. These anxieties shouldn't stop you, though, from attaining the full potential of your organization.

## Some of the finest strategies to overcome financial worry and go on with confidence:

### 1. Understand your money.
Before you can overcome your financial anxieties, you must confront them. Begin by knowing your company's financial status. This entails examining your cash flow, costs, and income streams.

If you're not familiar with numbers, engaging with an accountant to guide you through the process might be beneficial. Once you've got a comprehensive view of your finances, you can start identifying areas for development and setting growth objectives.

## 2. Create a budget.

One of the most common causes of financial anxiety is the concern of not having enough money. To address this, try defining a budget for your company. A budget may help you keep track of your expenditures and ensure that your resources are allocated appropriately. Sticking to your budget gives you more control over your finances and helps you avoid overpaying.

## 3. Prepare for the worst.

Nobody enjoys thinking about worst-case scenarios, but planning for them is critical. Consider developing a contingency plan for your firm to provide a safety net in the event of an emergency. This might involve setting aside an emergency cash or devising a backup plan for staffing and operations. Additionally, consider purchasing company insurance to protect your assets and financial security.

## 4. Seek resources.

Financial management is a complicated subject, and seeking assistance and resources is acceptable. Look for local business development groups or online forums where you may network and learn from other entrepreneurs' experiences. Budgeting applications and calculators are among the financial planning tools and services available online. If you require support or guidance, please do not hesitate to ask.

## 5. Embrace change.

Businesses are continuously adapting and developing. Financial anxieties might be overwhelming and difficult, but they do not have to prevent you from developing and increasing. Embrace change and take measured risks to propel your company ahead. You may realize your company's full potential by remaining nimble and open to new chances.

## Understanding Fear of Money

Navigating the world of economics may be a daunting experience, especially for those transitioning into adulthood. One of the most common phobias associated with financial management is chrometophobia, or fear of money. This concern, while rarely mentioned, has a significant impact on how individuals, from teens to adults, perceive and manage their financial affairs.

Chrometophobia is more than just concern; it is a deep-seated dread that can impede progress toward financial freedom and well-being. This dread, which is typically based on unfamiliar or misunderstood aspects of money management, can lead to avoidance and financial immobility. However, knowing and facing this anxiety is the first step toward financial independence and confidence.

### Confronting Financial Fears

The quest to overcome chrometophobia begins with an honest appraisal of one's financial condition. Fear is sometimes caused by a lack of information or misconceptions about a subject. As a result, by casting light on your money by reviewing bank accounts, credit card bills, loans, and other financial commitments, you may dispel myths and lay a solid basis for educated decision-making. This clarity in knowing your financial situation is critical in removing anxieties and misconceptions.

• **Direct Financial Engagement:** Account balances and statements must be reviewed on a regular basis. Understanding your financial situation, whether comfortable or problematic, gives a clear beginning point for development.

• **Financial Reflection:** View your money as a travel map rather than a static image. Determine whether your present financial practices are helping you achieve your goals. If not, it may be time to set a new direction.

• **Mindset Shift:** Understand that financial wellness is a journey, not a destination. It requires ongoing learning and adaptability rather than a one-time repair.

**Building Financial Security**

Developing a sense of financial stability is an important step toward conquering your phobia of money. This security stems mostly from being prepared for unexpected events and making prudent borrowing selections.

• **Creating an Emergency Fund:** One of the most effective methods to fight financial worry is to start an emergency savings account. This fund serves as a financial cushion, offering peace of mind in the face of unforeseen events such as job loss or medical issues. Financial gurus often advocate saving three to six months' worth of living costs. Even tiny, consistent donations can accumulate into a sizable amount over time.

• **Smart Borrowing Practices:** If borrowing is required, proceed with prudence and understanding. Prioritize loans for critical investments like education or housing, and avoid high-risk or high-interest borrowing, particularly for depreciating items like vehicles. When deciding on a loan, evaluate interest rates, conditions, and customer evaluations to help you make a wise financial decision.

## Setting and Meeting Long-Term Financial Goals

After addressing urgent financial concerns, the next stage in ensuring a secure financial future is to establish long-term objectives.

• **Visualize Your Financial Future:** Consider where you want to be financially in the next ten, twenty, or thirty years. Whether it's buying a house, saving for retirement, or supporting personal aspirations like travel, having clear financial objectives is critical.

• **Strategic Financial Planning:** Once you've determined your goals, make a strategy to attain them. This might involve making monthly payments to retirement accounts such as 401(k)s or IRAs, investing in stocks, or pursuing other savings options. The goal is to start early and be consistent, as this technique helps you accumulate money over time and eliminates the need to take out debt for future costs.

## Seeking Professional Help as Needed

There is no shame in obtaining competent financial guidance. In reality, expert advice can frequently be the key to realizing your financial potential.

• **Consult with Financial Experts:** If you're having trouble with a specific element of your finances, such as debt reduction, budgeting, or long-term planning, try speaking with a financial adviser or a nonprofit credit counselor. These specialists may give specialized guidance and assist you in developing a complete plan to achieve your financial goals.

• **Mental Health and Financial Well-being:** If financial concerns are generating substantial stress or worry, it may be beneficial to consult with a mental health expert. Financial therapists specialize in the confluence of money and emotional well-being and can provide solutions for dealing with and overcoming long-held financial worries.

# CONCLUSION

As we reach the end of our journey through "Solving for Success: Crafting Wealth through Numerical Wisdom," it's time to reflect on the insights and strategies we've explored. We've delved into the foundational principles of financial success, built a robust framework for wealth accumulation, and uncovered advanced strategies to secure a prosperous future.

The essence of this book lies in the realization that financial success is not a matter of luck or chance but a systematic application of numerical wisdom. By understanding the equations that govern our financial decisions, setting clear and measurable goals, and implementing effective budgeting, saving, and investment strategies, we've learned to navigate the complexities of personal finance with confidence and precision.

"Solving for Success" is more than just a guide—it's a roadmap to financial independence and prosperity. By following the steps laid out, you have the potential to transform your financial landscape, achieve your dreams, and secure a future defined by abundance and stability. Your journey to financial mastery has just begun, and the possibilities are limitless. Embrace the challenge, apply the wisdom, and watch as your financial success unfolds.

www.ingramcontent.com/pod-product-compliance
Lightning Source LLC
Chambersburg PA
CBHW071957210526
45479CB00003B/970